POETRY
FROM the
HEART

PALMETTO

PUBLISHING

Charleston, SC

www.PalmettoPublishing.com

Hardcover ISBN: 9798822963245
Paperback ISBN: 9798822963252

POETRY FROM the HEART

By: Tina Rená Courtney Fisher

love

TABLE OF CONTENTS

THINKING OF YOU

My thoughts for today are focused
On you about our real love pure,
Honest and true.

I think of you each morning
And also, during the day,
I think of you constantly
In an extraordinary way.

While I think of you.,
I hope you think of me
And treasure our real love
with truth and honesty

TRUE FRIENDS

You were always there for me,
Even when I was too blind to see,
We've been through hell and back
So many times, I think I've lost track.

All we wanted was to have fun,
What we got was ridiculed and Shunned,
you loved your loves, And I loved mine,
 too bad we can't Blame that mess on
some cheap wine.

We took the bait we had some falls.
We walked before we learned to Crawl,
 now it's time to move on and,
 quit singing the same sad song.

Just remember you'll always be
Very special to me!

WISHES

I always wished you'd stay,
and never go away.
I wished for a love that would
Be strong but now it's just all gone.

I wished to the stars for a love,
Everlasting but I never knew how soon,
the shadows would be casting.

I still an always will wish you the best.

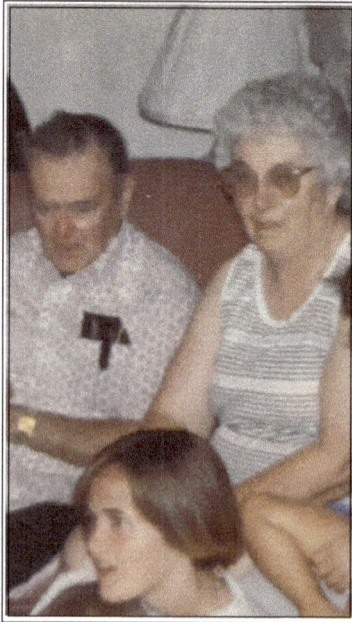

INSIDE MY HEART

Now I look inside my heart.
And all I can see is how it's torn a[part.
You were the first to hurt. Me quite this bad.
But that's OK, because for long I won't be sad.

The love we once shared.
Was strong and true.
And all I ever wanted was,
Was to be happy with you.

WAS IT

Well. I see you're laughing now.
But I still can't understand how.
I love you now. As I Loved. You then.
And that love won't stop, not
Even when you say when.

I should have left you. A long. Time ago.
But I just couldn't let you go.
Was everything you told me.
Was it just a lie? Was it all a joke?
Between you and I.

THE DAY YOU WERE BORN

The day you were born.
I knew you would be the best.
Thing that ever happened to me.

The day you were born.
All I could see was.
Your beautiful face.
Looking back at me.

As you grew, I also knew.
That you were going to make me.
So very proud of you.

I want you to know that, Mom.
Will always be here for you.
And so very proud, you see.

Because the day you were born.
You were always meant to be.

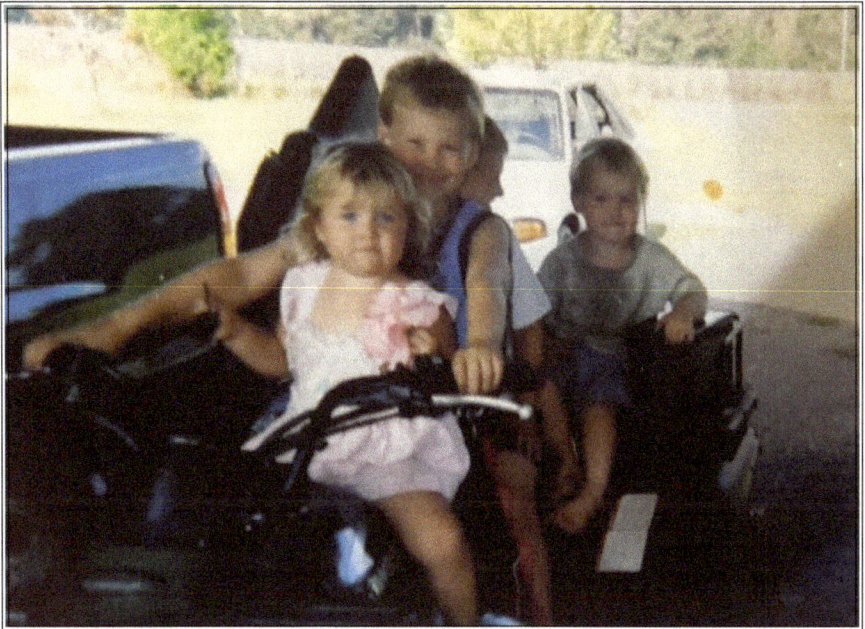

MOMENT

Yeah. The moment I saw you.
Is the moment I knew.
That the day would come.
That I would always Want to be.
With you.

But you're living your dream.
And so, it seems.
That I can't compete.
With these types of things.

A moment came.
When I should have spoke.
But all I did.
I became shy and choked.

I want you to see.
I'm the woman you need.
I'll stand by your side.
For an eternity.

AS I SIT

As I sit and talk to you.
I keep wondering if it is true?
That a man like you.
Could really see.
The me I always wanted to be.

As I sit, I think about.
What could I do?
To make you think about.
No doubt

Now. I ask could it be true?
That I was always meant. To be. With you.
And only you.

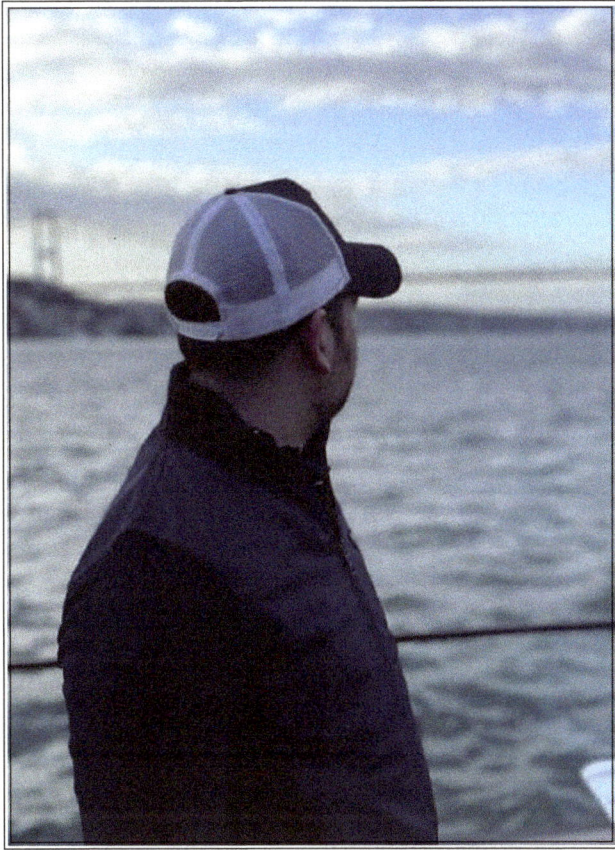

I LAY HERE

I lay here in a deep sleep.
And I hear nothing but a weep.

I can't wake.
But I can breathe.
Could this really be the end for me?

My eyes won't open.
God help me.
Is this my time?
Could it be?
The end of my lifeline.
So Unfair, you see.

As. I lay here so quiet. And still.
I pray to you, Lord
For your grace and strong will.

WHAT I WANT

What I want is you.,
To look me in my face It's true.
Because somehow in this crazy place.
I believe that God.
Made me just for you.

What I want? It's for you.
To see just how happy we could be.
I want you to always hold me,
I want you to kiss me,
Hell, I want you to sometimes
Even miss me.

I want so much from you
It's true, you stole my heart,
Right out of the blue.

Now all I want is my time with you
And maybe a happy ending
Too!

YOUR VOICE

When I was sick and in despair.
It was your voice.
It came from nowhere.

When I needed something.
To find my way.
And give me strength.
And my dismay.

I found it within.
You And your music? At a moment when.
I couldn't wake up. Until I heard,
Your voice sing to me,
Talking Tennessee once more?

DEDICATED TO YOU

There is one man.
God knows this is true.
And I need to dedicate this one to you.

From out of nowhere.
Your voice rang through.
This much I can honestly tell you.
Is absolutely true.

I had no name.,
I had no face,
But your music hit me.
In just the right place.

At the right time.
It's very true.
God sent grace. And.
He did it through you.

Your voice gave me strength.
When I needed it most,
because the cancer that.
Take me like an unwanted host.

Now cancer free.
I'm here to see.
My children grow old.
Because you made it so easy. To fight.

I focused on you.
And now I'm free.
No more cancer.
It didn't take me.

Now, I dedicate this one to you.
See, it was your voice.
Your voice that saved me is true.
That's why I dedicate this poem.
As a complete. Thank you.
Directly to you.

DETICATION to MY
KIDS
MOM
UN-NAMED

FOR YOU

MY WORLD, MY LIFE, MY KIDS

This book is a complete thank you and dedication to my children. Without all of you whether you knew it or not you're the reason this was able to happen. I am more blessed than anyone will ever know. Remember Mom LOVES YOU ALL!

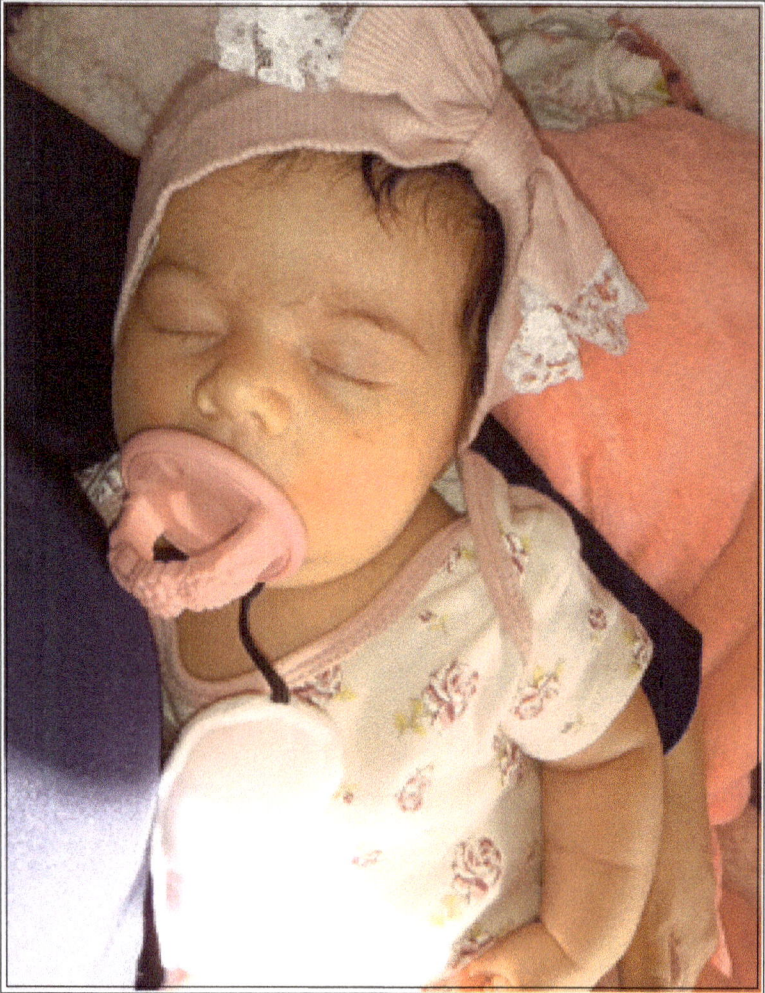

MOM

A special thank you to my mom! Even though I was that kid growing up that lashed out and stole from her and yes, I lied too, she never gave up on me and knew what I could do so. MOM yes you this one's for you as well I LOVE YOU!

DW

 Last but certainly not least to that one musician who helped save me. Your music is my power, and it fuels me so never stop pushing, people like me need music like yours to keep pushing through the worst of storms.

 So, thank you DW as you can see, I have a true love and connection to you through your music you see.

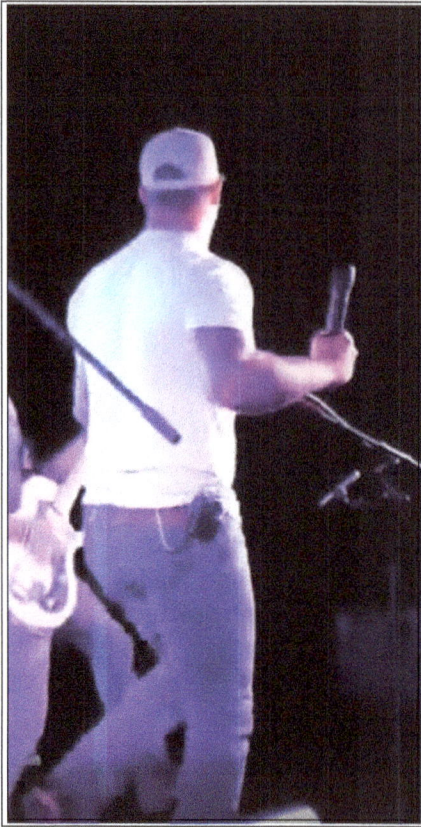

ABOUT THE AUTHOR

Tina Rena Courtney Fisher is a cancer survivor who has overcome dozens of surgeries, and who is currently living with a chronic illness. As a single mom, her children and grandchildren are her life, and they give her no end of joy. Tina is proud to have come as far as she has, and she is grateful to share her words as a reminder that a life lived authentically and bravely is always a life worth living—no matter what.

Milton Keynes UK
Ingram Content Group UK Ltd.
UKHW020217151124
451096UK00020B/247

9 798822 963252